HAIR-RAISING
MONSTER
STORIES

BY BRIANNA HALL

Consultant:
Simon J. Bronner
Distinguished Professor of American Studies and Folklore
Chair, American Studies Program
Pennsylvania State University

CAPSTONE PRESS
a capstone imprint

Snap Books are published by Capstone Press,
1710 Roe Crest Drive, North Mankato, Minnesota 56003
www.capstonepub.com

Library of Congress Cataloging-in-Publication Data
Cataloging-in-publication information is on file with the Library of Congress.
ISBN: 978-1-4296-9982-2 (library binding)
ISBN: 978-1-4765-3560-9 (ebook PDF)

Editorial Credits
Angie Kaelberer, editor; Ashlee Suker, designer; Wanda Winch, media
researcher; Jennifer Walker, production specialist

Photo Credits
Alamy: Dale O'Dell, 9; Alex Tomlinson, 23; AP Images: Tsunemi Kubodera
of the National Science Museum of Japan, HO, 28; The Bridgeman Art
Library: Private Collection/Gino D'Achille, 12; Corbis: Sygma/Kevin Dufy,
21; Dreamstime: Sergey Drozdov, 19; Fortean Picture Library, 5, 15, 25, 26, 31;
Mary Evans Picture Library, 17; Photo by Kimberly Woods, 6; Shutterstock:
andreiuc88, back cover, 3, Anthony Hall, 25 (bottom), C. Salisbury, 30,
echo3005, cover (brush strokes), Jeff Thrower, cover, 1 (monster), keren-seg,
2, 4, 8, 14, 18, 22, 24, Svitlana Kazachek, 20-21 (b), Yellowj, 12-13 (bkgrnd);
SuperStock Inc/Animals Animals, 11

Design elements:
Shutterstock: basel101658, tree branch silhouette, David M. Schrader, brush
frame, Emelyanov, fractal pattern, foxie, brush stroke photo captions,
happykanppy, green, blue water color, HiSunnySky, grey grunge frame, Igor
Shikov, green frame, javarman, tree frame, cloud background, kanate, olive
water color, Leksus Tuss, green scratch texture, Massimo Saivezzo, grunge
floral, yellow, mcherevan, chandelier, Neil Lang, black smudge border,
Nejron Photo, brown wall texture, optimarc, line brush texture, pashabo,
grunge brown, blue borders, Pixel 4 Images, trees section, Theeradech Sanin,
distressed wood frame

Quote on page 13 courtesy:
Napier, John. *Bigfoot: The Yeti and Sasquatch in Myth and Reality.*
New York, E. P. Dutton & Co., Inc., 1973, pages 39–40.

Table of Contents

Modern Monster History..............................4

Apemen..8

American Horrors...................................14

Dino-Monsters..18

The Death Worm...................................22

From the Deep......................................24

Monster Hunters...................................30

Read More...32

Internet Sites.......................................32

Chapter One

Modern Monster History

Chupacabra

Imagine you are napping on a summer afternoon. Your mom rushes into your room and shakes you awake. "Get up! You have to see this animal!" she says. You stumble to your feet and look out the window. You pinch yourself to make sure you are not dreaming. But even after you do, it remains.

Don't think it will ever happen to you? Madelyne Tolentino of Canóvanas, Puerto Rico, didn't either. But now she believes in the vampire monster El Chupacabra.

El Chupacabra means "the goat sucker" in Spanish. People say that the monster drains its victims' blood.

Tolentino describes the creature she saw outside her mother's home as being about 3 feet (1 meter) tall and walking on two legs. It had human hands with long fingers. Its eyes were big and slanted. Two little dots were in the place where a nose should have been. The creature was mostly bald and had spikes down its spine. Tolentino said it skipped like a kangaroo without seeming to touch the ground.

Some people believe this photo is a chupacabra. Others say it's only a dog with a skin disease.

Tolentino reported seeing the Chupacabra in 1995, but it remains a mystery. No one knows where it came from or where it hides. No one even knows what it is. Some people claim the Chupacabra is a diseased animal. Others believe it is a secret government experiment gone wrong.

Many farmers believe the Chupacabra drinks the blood of other creatures. Puerto Rican farmer Don Franciso Ruiz discovered three of his goats and their young dead. The animals didn't have a drop of blood in their bodies.

Another farmer, Celso Rabello of Brazil, found nine of his pigs drained of blood in spring 1999. The predator left no tracks, and the lock on the animals' enclosure hadn't been broken. Could it have been the chupacabra?

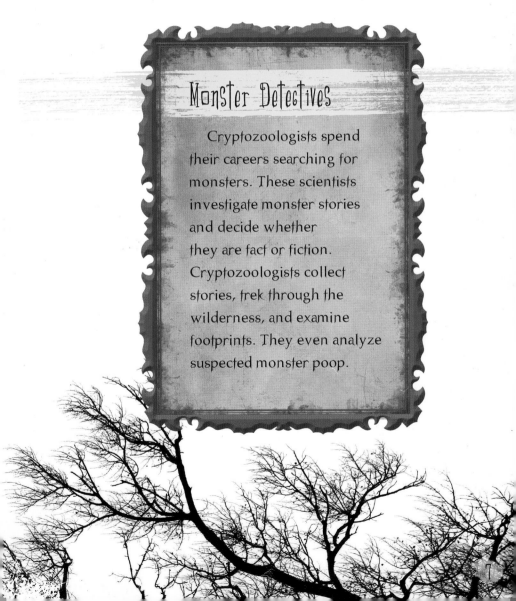

Monster Detectives

Cryptozoologists spend their careers searching for monsters. These scientists investigate monster stories and decide whether they are fact or fiction. Cryptozoologists collect stories, trek through the wilderness, and examine footprints. They even analyze suspected monster poop.

Chapter Two

Apemen

Bigfoot of the Woods

In 1924 lumberjack Albert Ostman set off on foot into the Canadian wilderness to pan for gold. Several nights into his journey, he awoke with a start. Ostman opened his eyes but couldn't see anything but the inside of his sleeping bag. His body jostled back and forth.

Ostman realized that something was carrying him like a giant sack of potatoes. When he was dropped to the ground, Ostman feared the worst. Ostman rolled out of the bag to find four hairy, curious faces looking down at him.

Ostman had heard stories of Bigfoot, but now he stood face to face with an entire Bigfoot family. The mother had wide hips and walked clumsily like a goose. The father stood 8 feet (2.4 m) tall. The parents and two children were covered in thick, coarse hair. Ostman feared for his life, but the family didn't harm him.

Six days passed before Ostman escaped the Bigfoot family's forest home. Lucky for him, he lived to tell the tale.

Most Bigfoot sightings have been in the Pacific Northwest region of North America.

Researcher Roger Patterson wanted to prove Bigfoot existed. In 1967 Patterson planned a trip with his friend Bob Gimlin to Six Rivers National Forest in California. His goal was to film Bigfoot.

On the afternoon of October 20, Patterson and Gimlin were on horseback as they neared a bank of a shallow creek. They stopped dead in their tracks. A Bigfoot stood on the opposite bank. It was 7 feet (2.1 m) tall and covered in black hair. Shaking, Patterson jumped off his horse, grabbed his camera, and started filming. The creature glared over its shoulder at the men, then stalked slowly into the woods. Some people think the film is just a person in a gorilla suit. Others, including some scientists, believe it is real.

Roger Patterson took a famous film of Bigfoot in 1967.

The Mountain Monster

Large, apelike men and women are said to walk all corners of Earth. They are known by more than 150 different names. In Alaska and Canada, the creature is called Sasquatch. In Siberia, Russia, it's Almas. In the Himalayan Mountains of Nepal, people know it as the Yeti.

Some say Yeti's can weigh up to 400 pounds (181 kilograms).

The Yeti's story begins in prehistoric times. Ancient people of the Himalayas believed the Yeti protected them from mountain demons. But they also viewed the Yeti as a clever trickster who stole food and livestock.

N. A. Tombazi, an English scientist and photographer, traveled to the Himalayas in 1924. He saw a curious creature walking upright through the snow.

The figure then walked out of view, but Tombazi was curious. He searched for more clues. The creature's footprints were shaped like a man's. They were 6 to 7 inches (15 to 18 centimeters) long and 4 inches (10 cm) wide.

But Tombazi's wasn't the last sighting of a Yeti. In fall 2012, fishermen and a forest worker claimed to have seen furry, humanlike creatures in Siberia. The creatures quickly disappeared into the wild after being spotted.

Chapter Three

American Horrors

Mothman: Messenger of Death

If Mothman pays you a visit, beware. The creature was first sighted on November 15, 1966, near Point Pleasant, West Virginia. Two young couples drove through the dark along the marshes of the Ohio River. Their names were Steve and Mary Mallette and Roger and Linda Scarberry.

Suddenly something huge loomed on the road. It had massive wings and stood 7 feet (2.1 m) tall. It stared at them with glowing red eyes. The driver stepped on the gas, but the creature followed. The car sped up to 100 miles (161 kilometers) per hour. But the frightened couples could still see the creature swooping alongside the car. It disappeared after they reached the Point Pleasant city limits.

Investigator John Keel traveled to Point Pleasant to learn about the Mothman. In 1975 he wrote a book about his experiences.

Terror gripped Point Pleasant as more people reported sightings of the strange creature. It appeared only at night—its red eyes ablaze. One woman said she saw the birdlike creature in her backyard. Three people claimed to see it near an abandoned TNT mine. A newspaper reporter called the creature "Mothman," and the name stuck. More than 100 people from Point Pleasant received a visit from Mothman—but why?

Exactly 13 months after the first sighting, a deadly disaster hit the town. Forty-six people died in the Silver Bridge collapse. After the tragedy, the Mothman sightings stopped. It seems the messenger of death completed its mission.

Jersey Devil:
The Ultimate Sibling Rivalry

ave you ever been so mad at your siblings that you wanted to ... eat them? That's unlikely. But this is the center of the Jersey Devil's chilling legend. Meet Mowas Leeds. This woman lived in New Jersey's countryside in the early 1700s with her husband and 12 children. She couldn't stand the thought of having another child. She said she would rather give birth to a monster than to another baby.

Mrs. Leeds' curse came true. Her final child was reportedly born with tall, batlike wings and glowing eyes. It had claws and hooves. Mrs. Leeds claimed the baby ate her other children. It escaped through the chimney and blazed a trail of terror through the countryside.

More than 200 years later, residents of New Jersey's Pine Barrens still say they see the devil child's spirit. A park ranger named John Irwin says he locked eyes with the haunting creature in 1993. Irwin was making his rounds through Wharton State Forest when a creature walked out of the woods.

More than 1,000 people reported seeing the Jersey Devil during January 1909.

Irwin said the monster stood upright and was more than

6 feet (1.8 m) tall. It had black fur that was wet and matted.

When the creature turned its head, Irwin saw two red eyes.

Sightings of the Jersey Devil continue to this day. But no one

has found proof of the monster's existence—not yet, anyway.

Chapter Four

Dino-Monsters

The Boatbreaker

North and South America are the home of bloodthirsty beasts, giant apemen, and cursed flyers. The swamps and jungles of Africa hide another sort of monster—living dinosaurs.

Anglers and river travelers of southeastern Africa keep their eyes peeled for Kongamato, which means "the breaker of boats." According to legend, anyone who looks into Kongamato's eyes dies. People say the creature looks much like a prehistoric reptile called a pterosaur. Its wingspan extends about 4 to 7 feet (1.2 to 2.1 m).

The pterosaur became extinct about 65 million years ago.

In Zimbabwe a man traveled by canoe alone into the swamplands. He staggered back with the following frightful story. The man's name is lost to the history books, but the year was 1925. The snake-infested swamplands stretched in front of the man as he fished from his canoe. Suddenly the man saw a red blur splash into the water near the canoe. A moment later he felt a long, pointed beak launch him into the air. Sharp pains ripped through his chest as he crashed into the water. He escaped the swamp and staggered back home. Hundreds of other fishermen were not so lucky.

The River Beast

Mokele-Mbembe is a force of nature—it stops the flow of rivers. This African dino-monster is said to be 15 to 30 feet (4.6 to 9 m) long. It is as tall as a jungle tree. A horn extends from its head. It swishes its tail like a crocodile.

Mokele-Mbembe haunts murky jungle swamps, rivers, and lakes. It frightens hippos and elephants with a howling roar. A swipe from its long neck could knock a person out cold.

In 1925 14-year-old Firman Mosomele was paddling a canoe on the Likouala aux Herbes River. The river was near his home in the People's Republic of Congo. A small head rose from the water near his canoe. Mosomele paddled toward it. The head continued rising out of the water. It rose 6 feet (1.8 m) atop a smooth, skinny neck. In terror, Mosomele quickly paddled away.

Nearly 60 years after Mosomele's experience, a group of scientists set out to find the monster. Their 1983 trip focused on Lake Tele, a huge lake hidden deep in the jungle.

Leader Marcellin Agnagna was filming monkeys near the shore with his camera. Then he heard one of the guides shout at him.

The man pointed to a round hump floating near the lake's center. A 6-foot (1.8-m) neck extended from the hump. Agnagna tried to keep his hands steady as he filmed the creature. After 20 minutes, the creature disappeared into the lake.

Agnagna's developed film returned completely black. Agnagna says he forgot to remove the camera's lens cap. Maybe the humid jungle air destroyed the film. Or is Agnagna hiding something? The world may never know, but Agnagna has stuck to his story.

A creature that may be Mokele-Mbembe was photographed in the Congo in 1981.

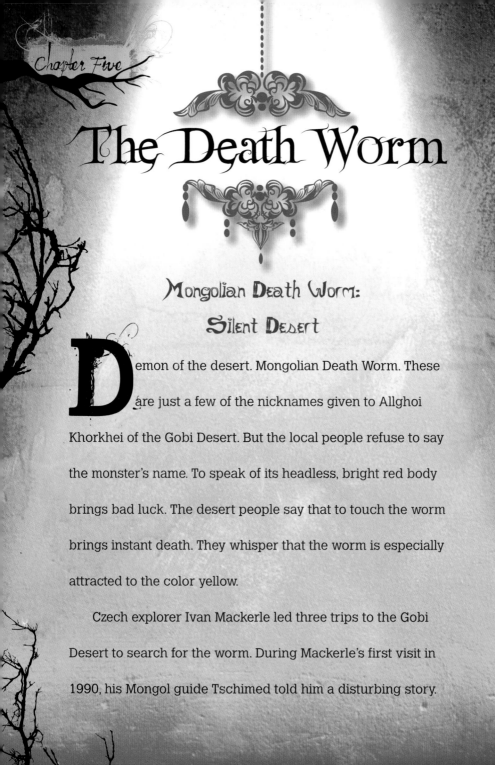

Chapter Five

The Death Worm

Mongolian Death Worm:
Silent Desert

Demon of the desert. Mongolian Death Worm. These are just a few of the nicknames given to Allghoi Khorkhei of the Gobi Desert. But the local people refuse to say the monster's name. To speak of its headless, bright red body brings bad luck. The desert people say that to touch the worm brings instant death. They whisper that the worm is especially attracted to the color yellow.

Czech explorer Ivan Mackerle led three trips to the Gobi Desert to search for the worm. During Mackerle's first visit in 1990, his Mongol guide Tschimed told him a disturbing story.

The worm's name means "intestine worm" in the Mongolian language. The worm's body looks like a human intestine.

A nomad boy played with his toys inside his tent. The boy turned his back. A worm stretching 5 feet (1.5 m) long and 1 foot (0.3 m) wide then squirmed from the sand. It rolled inside the tent and wriggled into the boy's yellow toy box. When the boy reached into his box, he was killed instantly. Some people think the worm killed the boy by electric shock. Others believe it spit poisonous venom like a snake.

This disturbing story is the closest Mackerle ever came to the Death Worm. The creature's mystery still haunts the huge desert.

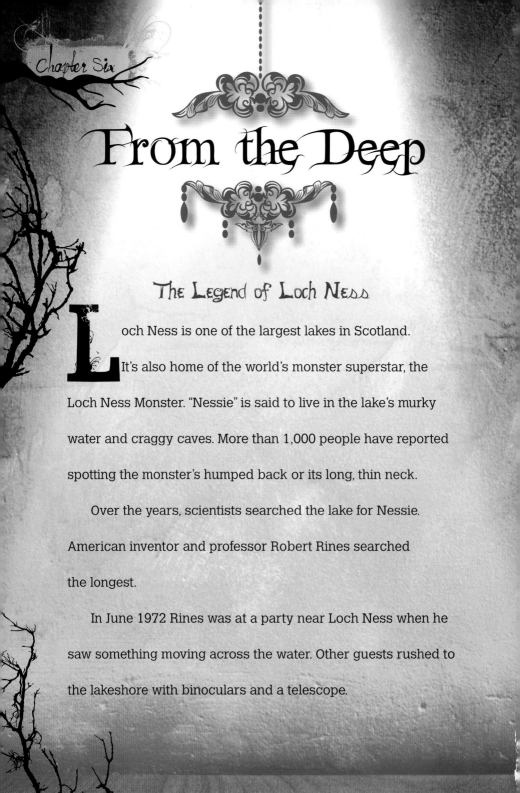

Chapter Six

From the Deep

The Legend of Loch Ness

Loch Ness is one of the largest lakes in Scotland. It's also home of the world's monster superstar, the Loch Ness Monster. "Nessie" is said to live in the lake's murky water and craggy caves. More than 1,000 people have reported spotting the monster's humped back or its long, thin neck.

Over the years, scientists searched the lake for Nessie. American inventor and professor Robert Rines searched the longest.

In June 1972 Rines was at a party near Loch Ness when he saw something moving across the water. Other guests rushed to the lakeshore with binoculars and a telescope.

Real or fake? People believe this image, taken in 1977, proves Nessie is real.

They saw a gray hump measuring about 25 feet (7.6 m) across with skin like an elephant's. It swam into the current and then reversed its direction. Then it vanished into the lake.

Rines was hooked. He led several trips to search for the monster. He used sonar, mini submarines, and underwater photography.

His most successful trip happened shortly after his search began. Rines believed his photos showed Nessie's true form—a cream-colored underbelly, a long neck, and a narrow head.

Rines last visited Loch Ness in 2008. He died the next year at age 87—still not having proved his theory about the mysterious monster.

Stories of the fearsome kraken date to the 1400s in Scandinavia.

Kraken: Mystery Solved

Most monster stories are unsolved mysteries. The story of the Kraken is an exception.

Two Norwegian fishermen sailed into the cold Norwegian Sea in the late 1600s. The waters around their boat filled with thick slime. A strong, nasty odor filled the air. The fishermen saw reddish armlike limbs rippling beneath the surface of the water. The fishermen tried to sail away but failed. A long, thin tentacle reached out of the water. It crushed the boat's front, plunging the men into the sea. They survived by clinging to the boat's wreckage. People in other parts of the world also told stories about the deadly sea monsters. In 1735 Swedish scientist Carl Linnaeus gave the monster a name—the kraken.

The Kraken story resurfaced in the 1870s when bizarre remains washed up on beaches around the world. They looked like squid, but were equipped to fight. Suckers ringed with small claws lined their eight arms. They had sharp, beaklike mouths. Strangest of all were the creature's eyes. They measured up to 12 inches (30 cm) across—about the size of a large pizza. Scientists gave it a Latin name—*Architeuthis*, or giant squid.

It wasn't until December 2006 that scientists observed the creature alive. Japanese scientist Tsunemi Kubodera led a trip to the Ogasawara Islands in the South Pacific. Kubodera chose these islands because they are feeding grounds of sperm whales, which eat giant squid.

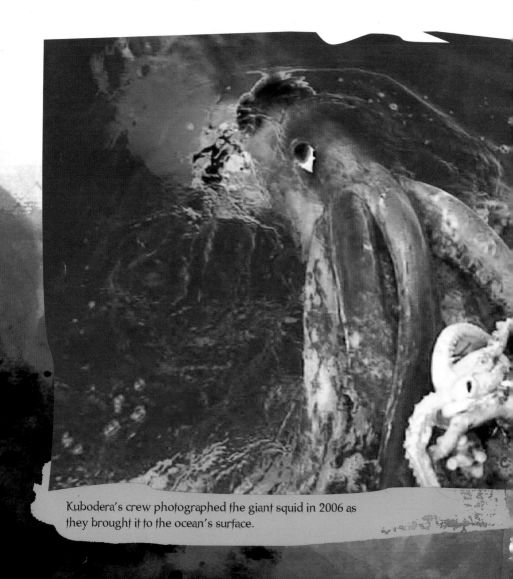

Kubodera's crew photographed the giant squid in 2006 as they brought it to the ocean's surface.

The crew sent a hook baited with small squid down into the ocean. A 24-foot (7.3-m) female squid attacked the squid bait, but became trapped in the line. The red squid rose to the surface. It thrashed about the boat as it tried to break free. Researchers filmed the squid from the boat's deck.

In July 2012, Kubodera and his crew used a small submarine to film another giant squid about 3,000 feet (914 m) beneath the sea. It was the first time the huge animal had been seen in its native habitat. The Kraken's tale—and Kubodera's research—shows that monsters can hide just beyond our prying eyes.

Monster Hunters

Cryptozoologists scour the Earth for hidden creatures. Yet, the majority of monster encounters happen to ordinary people. Albert Ostman never asked for a vacation with a Bigfoot family. Firman Mosomele never asked to see Mokele-Mebembe's hulking shape. Some people may chalk up these monster stories to excitement and lies, but what of the thousands of other sightings in the world? The monster search is short on evidence, but eyewitness accounts can't be ignored.

So if you find yourself on a hike, train your eyes to the distant woods. If you drive through a rural field, scan the skies. If you paddle a deep lake, look closely at the water. You never know who—or what—you may find.

READ MORE

Emmer, Rick. *Mokele-Mbembe: Fact or Fiction?* Creature Science Investigation. New York: Chelsea House, 2010.

Hawkins, John. *Bigfoot and Other Monsters.* Mystery Hunters. New York: PowerKids Press, 2012.

Newquist, H. P. *Here There Be Monsters: Legendary Kraken and the Giant Squid.* New York: Houghton Mifflin, 2010.

Yomtov, Nel. *Tracking Sea Monsters, Bigfoot, and Legendary Beasts.* Unexplained Phenomena. Mankato, Minn.: Capstone Press, 2011.

INTERNET SITES

FactHound offers a safe, fun way to find Internet sites related to this book. All of the sites on FactHound have been researched by our staff.

Here's all you do:

Visit *www.facthound.com*

Type in this code: 9781429699822

 Check out projects, games and lots more at **www.capstonekids.com**

TITLES IN THIS SET: